My School Art Journal

By: Leslie Kay Brown
The Art Gypsy

ISBN 9781722972523

kindle direct publishing

Copyrigt 2018
Leslie Brown

www.ArtGypsyDecals.com

Art Journal Journey

Hello,

I'm glad you took this path. You are going on an art discovery. This journal will take you through all the basics of art and drawing. You will learn a little art history and some fun facts! This book covers things like drawing faces, perspective, and shading.

Have some fun...

Remember, everyone was a beginner at some point.

— Leslie

ART HACKS

Did someone say BLEED?

DON'T USE MARKERS OR PAINT IN THIS JOURNAL... IT WIL BLEED THROUGH!!!

DRAW LIGHT-
It's really anoying when you rip the paper to shreds with the eraser!

TRACING is OK for practice but we all know when you are trying to claim stuff you stole...

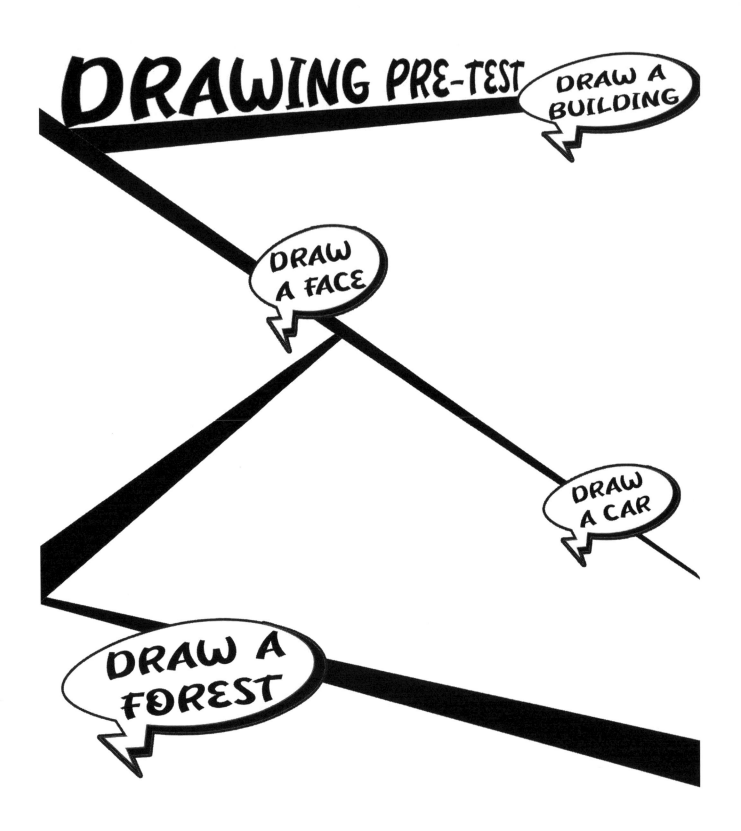

ELEMENTS OF ART
Cheat Sheet.........

COLOR — CREATES MOOD
WARM-COOL-NEUTRAL-ETC.

LINE — THIN-THICK-WAVY
JAGGED-DASHED-ETC.

SHAPE — GEOMETRIC-ORGANIC

FORM — 3-D REAL OR ILLUSION

VALUE — LIGHTNESS OR DARKNESS
AND ALL THE SHADES IN BETWEEN

SPACE — 3D - DEPTH-DIMENISHING
SIZE-OVERLAPPING

TEXTURE — ROUGH-SMOOTH
SLIMY-FURRY

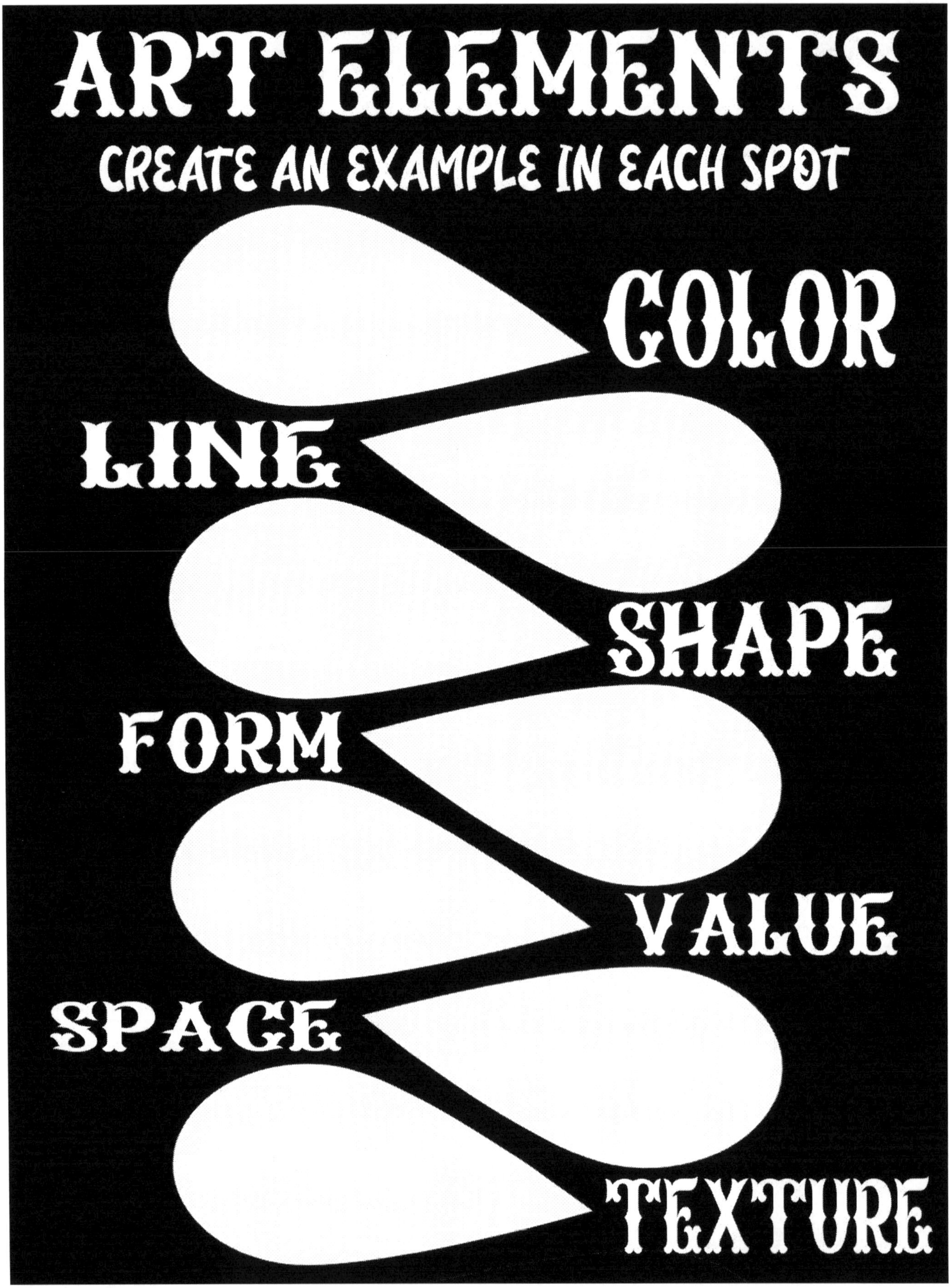

ART ELEMENTS

CREATE AN EXAMPLE IN EACH SPOT

COLOR

LINE

SHAPE

FORM

VALUE

SPACE

TEXTURE

Art-I-Facts

Frans Marc was such an ugly baby his father fainted when he saw him!

*Wanted to become a Priest, Philosopher, and finally settled on Artist.

*Drafted into the German army in World War I in 1914

*After mobilization of the German Army, the government identified notable artists to be withdrawn from combat for their own safety. Marc was on the list but was struck in the head and killed instantly by a shell splinter during the Battle of Verdun in 1916 before orders for reassignment could reach him.

QUOTE- "Van Gogh is for me the most authentic, the greatest, the most poignant painter I know. To paint a bit of the most ordinary nature, putting all one's faith and longings into it – that is the supreme achievement... Now I paint... only the simplest things... Only in them are the symbolism, the pathos, and the mystery of nature to be found."

COLOR

PRIMARY COLORS
YELLOW
BLUE
RED

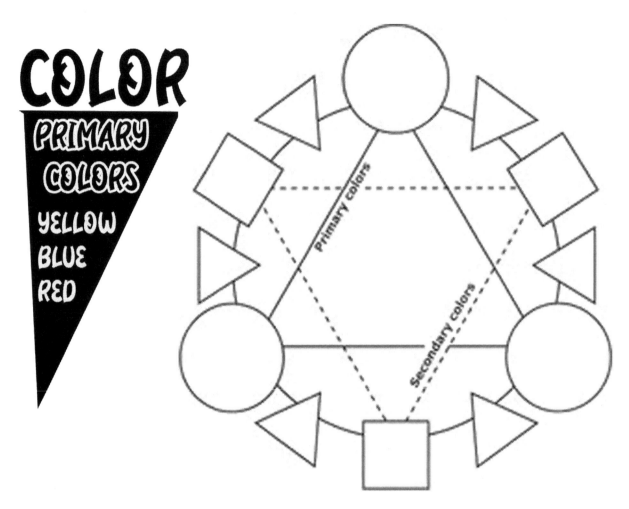

You can use the primary colors to make all the other colors on the color wheel.

you can try the blending with paint on a seperate paper to see what the colors make and then color in this chart.

You might only want to use colored pencil here.

Color in the ⭕ with the 3 primary colors.

Color in the ⬜ with the 3 secondary colors
PURPLE, GREEN, ORANGE.

Color the △ with the colors that have 2 names-
RED-ORANGE, BLUE-GREEN, etc.

Notice it's the 2 colors on either side of the △

Color Theory

RED
HOT
ANGER
DANGER
STOP

BLUE-CALM-PEACE-NATURE

warm and cool colors create a mood

COMPLIMENTARY
opposites on the color wheel

RED-GREEN
BLUE-ORANGE
PURPLE-YELOW

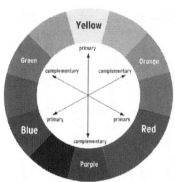

COMPLIMENTARY- "oh, you look so good!!!

Opposites do attract, these pairs make each other look good.
Why do you thing they seem so familliar?
What logos use these colors?

WARNING- if you mix these colors- as in paint- they dull each
other down and also can make shades of BROWN
So if you run out of brown paint- make your own!

HUE- the name of the color
VALUE- how light or dark a color is

Color Value

Pure Hue + White = Tint
Pure Hue + Black & White = Tone
Pure Hue + Black = Shade

In 1900 Homer sent The Gulf Stream to Philadelphia to be exhibited at the Pennsylvania Academy of the Fine Arts, and after it was returned later that year he wrote "I have painted on the picture since it was in Philadelphia & improved it very much (more of the Deep Sea water than before)." In fact, comparison with an early photograph of the painting shows that Homer not only reworked the ocean, but changed the starboard gunwale by breaking it, added the sail and the red dash of color near the waterline, made the boat's name (Anna – Key West) clearly legible, and painted in the ship at the upper left horizon, possibly to mitigate the sense of desolation in the work. He then showed the painting at the Carnegie Institute in Pittsburgh, and asked $4,000 for it.

List the things that are going on in this painting...

In the water _____

On the water _____

Far away _____

On the boat _____

Why on earth could that man just be chillin' out on deck? _____

_____

CRITIQUE

**THE GULF STREAM
WINSLOW HOMER
1899
OIL ON CANVAS
Metropolitan Museum
of Art
in New York City**

DESCRIPTION
Describe this art as if you were talking to someone who couln't see it.

ANALASIS
what ELEMENTS of art are used to make the artwork?
LINE, COLOR, SHAPE, TEXTURE, FORM, VALUE, SACE
what PRINCIPALS of art are used to make the artwork?
EMPPHASIS, RHYTHM/MOVEMENT, UNITY REPETITION/PATTERN, CONTRAST/VARIETY, BALANCE, PROPORTION

INTERRETATION
1. Does the work make you think or feel?
2. Do you think this work was successful/why?
3. How does this work relate to the world you've experienced?

JUDGEMENT
1. Give your opinion on the works achievement or failure.
2. Is the work unique?
3. What could have improved the work?

DESCRIPTION, ANALASIS, INTERPRETATION, JUDGEMENT

D _____

A _____

I _____

J _____

Don't use lots of words... get to the point.

DRAWING TIPS

SIZE MATTERS

WOW! Those cactusesses look far away

DRAW BIGGER= CLOSER
DRAW SMALER= FARTHER AWAY

DRAW FURTHER DOWN ON THE PAGE TO LOOK CLOSER

THE MOUNTAINS GET LIGHTER SHOWING THEY ARE FAR AWAY

NOW YOU TRY AND DRAW SOMETHING....SHOW THE SIZE RELATIONSHIP

OVERLAPPING

and running off the edge of the page.

What kind of crazy talk is that?

It's actually a good thing..

OVERLAPPING- shows that one object is in front of another, it creates DEPTH

RUN OFF- creates the sense that the art continues beyond the page.

DRAW SOMETHING BELOW THAT DOES BOTH

Iteration practice
Draw a different version of the object here in each square.

DEADLY	ROTTEN	MAGICAL
HAUNTED	**EXPENSIVE**	**HOLIDAY**
TALKING	**VAMPIRE**	**FRIGHTENED**

WARM-UP

ARTIST NAME
GEORGE RODRIGUE

ARTWORK NAME
WE WILL RISE AGAIN

DATE OF ART
2005

NATIONALITY
AMERICAN

BORN
1944-2013

http://www.georgerodrigue.com/

I worked with the famous artist, George Rodrigue on the first Scotty Book. My students learned all about George's "Blue Dog" art and used our school pet- a dog named Scotty to be the spokesdog in our books. No Dog Left Behind teaches people to evacuate their pets during a disaster.. We went on to create several more Scotty books. All of the paintings were created under my supervision in the art class by 5th-8th graders. Kids really learned how to paint & each picture was 3 feet square!

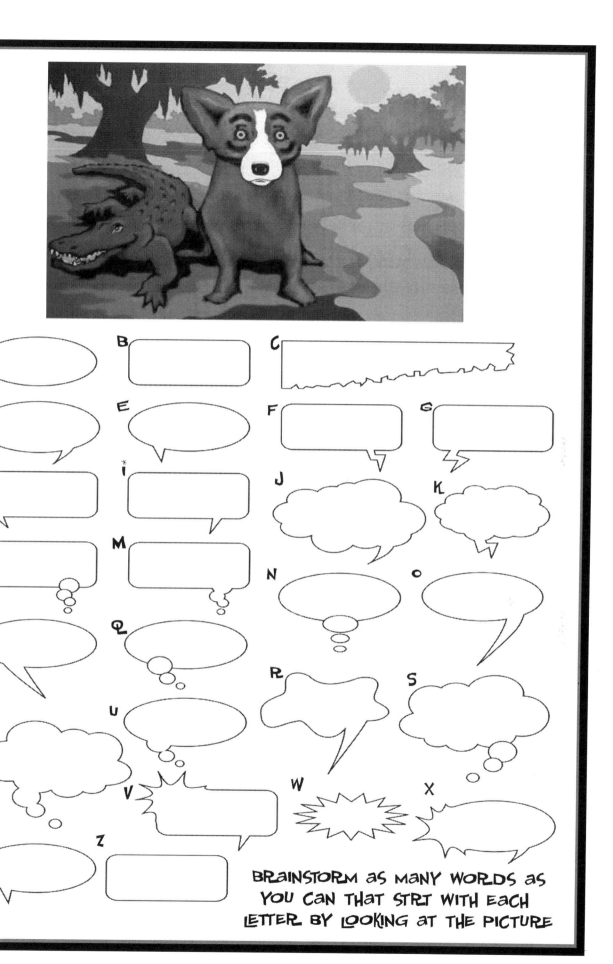

BRAINSTORM AS MANY WORDS AS YOU CAN THAT STRT WITH EACH LETTER BY LOOKING AT THE PICTURE

George Rodrigue created "blue dog"

DRAW SCOTTY HERE

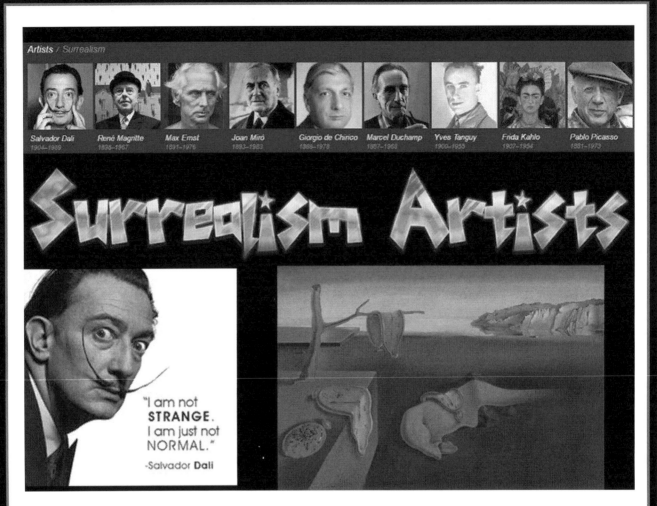

SUR·RE·AL·ISM
səˈrēəˌlizəm/ noun

a 20th-century avant-garde movement in art and literature that sought to release the creative potential of the unconscious mind, for example by the irrational juxtaposition of images.

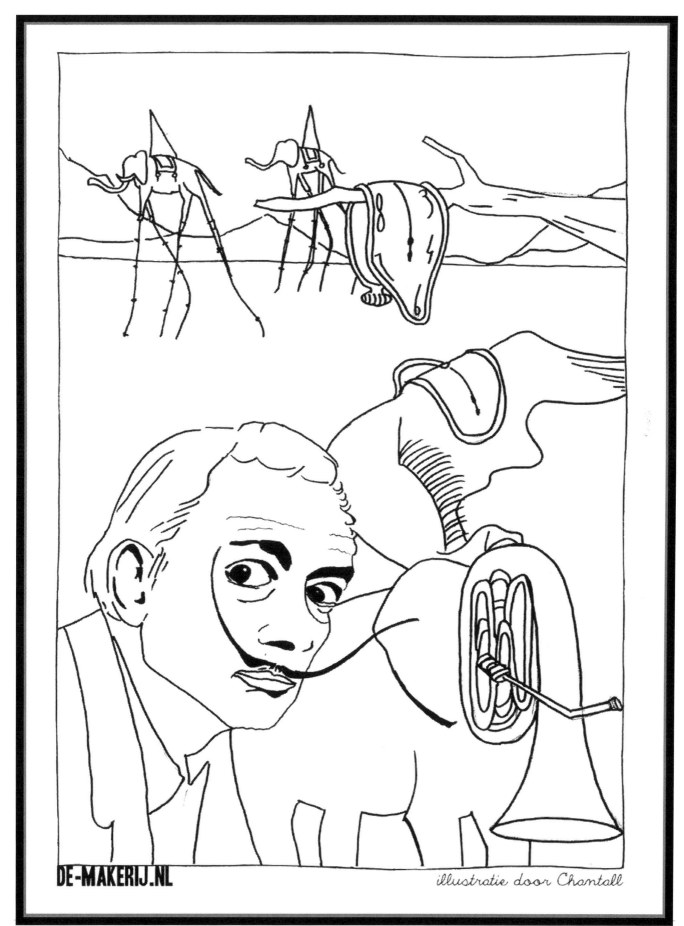

THE SON OF MAN
Artist
René Magritte
Year 1964
Type Oil on canvas
Dimensions
45.67 in × 35 in
Location Private Collection

Surrealism in visual art is usually very strange, odd and the concept may not make sense. Although surreal paintings contain identifiable objects that are not abstract, certain aspects of the painting may be warped or disfigured and often have an odd arrangement of objects that would never be seen together in real life.

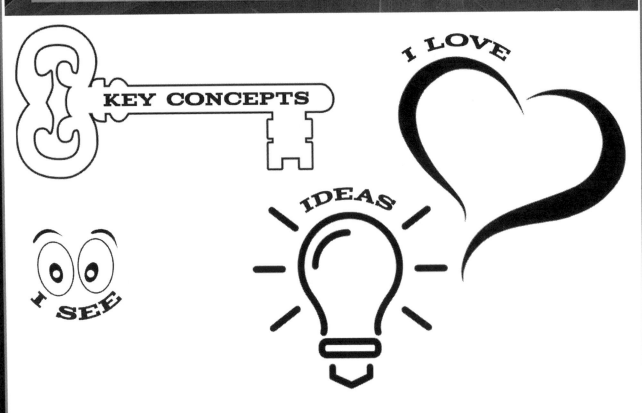

KEY CONCEPTS

I LOVE

I SEE

IDEAS

VALUE IS THE **LIGHTNESS OR DARKNESS** OF TONES OR COLORS. WHITE IS THE LIGHTEST VALUE; BLACK IS THE DARKEST. THE VALUE HALFWAY BETWEEN THESE EXTREMES IS CALLED MIDDLE GRAY.

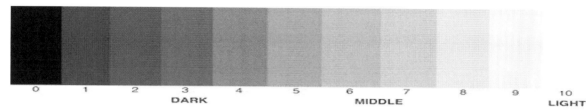

MAKE THE MOST AMAZING - CREATIVE VALUE CHART EVER....

El Dia de los Muertos
ARTIST NAME
RUFINO TAMAYO

DATE OF ART 1980
NATIONALITY
MEXICAN
BORN 1899
DIED 1991

Tamayo's 1970 painting *Tres Personajes* was bought by a Houston man as a gift for his wife in 1977, then stolen from their storage locker in 1987 during a move. In 2003, Elizabeth Gibson found the painting in the trash on a New York City curb. Gibson and the former owner arranged to sell the painting at a Sotheby's auction. In November, 2007 Gibson received a $15,000 reward plus a portion of the $1,049,000 auction sale price.

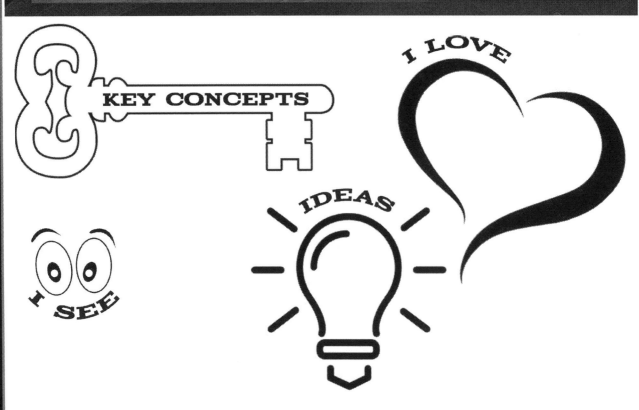

WARM-UP

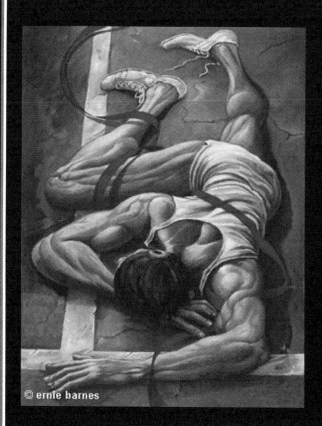

ARTIST NAME

ERNIE BARNES

ARTWORK NAME

HIS EFFORT

DATE OF ART

2007?

NATIONALITY

AFRICAN AMERICAN

BORN

1938-2009

PAINTER FOR "GOOD TIMES" TV SHOW & PRO FOOTBALL PLAYER

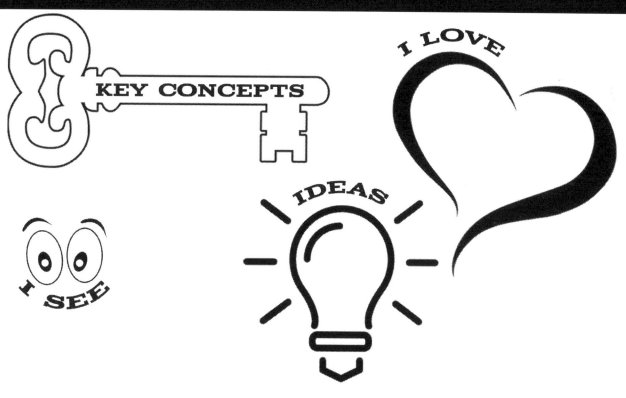

KEY CONCEPTS

I LOVE

I SEE

IDEAS

FORESHORTENING

The Ernie Barnes painting uses FORESHORTNING-
Drawing a part of something like it is smaller on one end
to make one end look closer to the viewer.

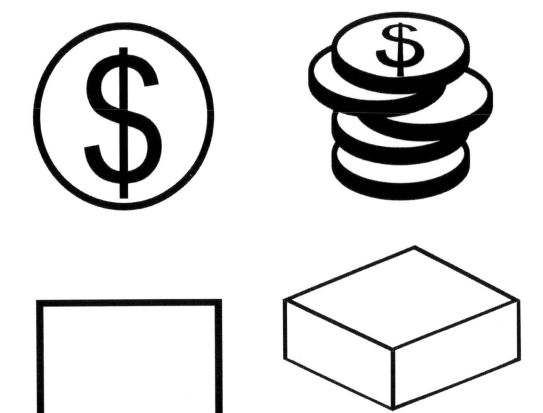

Practice drawing FORESHORTENED circles and squares...
CYLINDERS & CUBES
on the next page.
Can you stack boxes like the coins?

ARTIST

ARTIST NAME

DUBRAVKO KRIZANIC "DUCK"

ARTWORK NAME

NEW BEETLE

DATE OF ART

2007

NATIONALITY

CROATIAN

BORN

1969

 TWO-DIMENSIONAL FORM CONSTRUCTS THE ILLUSION OF 3D IN 2D MEDIA BY A SKILFUL MANIPULATION OF THE VISUAL ELEMENTS.

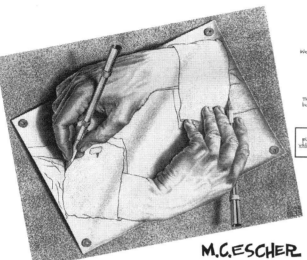

M.C. ESCHER

The Illusion of Space: Shading

We use LINE to create VALUE.

VALUE is: _____

This is a value scale, showing 8 degrees of gray between white and black.

When we shade, we:
* go light to dark
* follow the contour of the object
* vary the pressure on our pencil

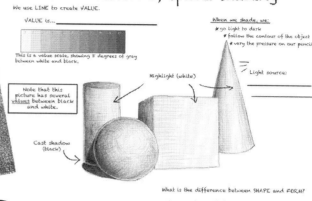

Note that this picture has several *values* between black and white.

Highlight (white)

Cast shadow (black)

Light source: _____

What is the difference between SHAPE and FORM?

_____

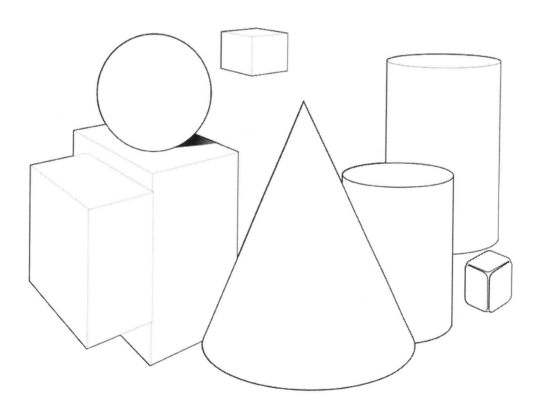

HERE IS A GROUP PROJECT CRATED BY KINDERGARDEN STUDENTS INSPIRED BY THE ARTIST PIET MONDRIAN

CREATE A MONDRIAN COLLAGE OR DRAWING

USE ONLY- PRIMARY COLORS + BLACK

WHAT ARE THE 3 PRIMARY COLORS?

_____   _____   _____

100 Things I Want To Draw

1. ____
2. ____
3. ____
4. ____
5. ____
6. ____
7. ____
8. ____
9. ____
10. ____
11. ____
12. ____
13. ____
14. ____
15. ____
16. ____
17. ____
18. ____
19. ____
20. ____
21. ____
22. ____
23. ____
24. ____
25. ____
26. ____
27. ____
28. ____
29. ____
30. ____
31. ____
32. ____
33. ____
34. ____
35. ____
36. ____
37. ____
38. ____
39. ____
40. ____
41. ____
42. ____
43. ____
44. ____
45. ____
46. ____
47. ____
48. ____
49. ____
50. ____
51. ____
52. ____
53. ____
54. ____
55. ____
56. ____
57. ____
58. ____
59. ____
60. ____
61. ____
62. ____
63. ____
64. ____
65. ____
66. ____
67. ____
68. ____
69. ____
70. ____
71. ____
72. ____
73. ____
74. ____
75. ____
76. ____
77. ____
78. ____
79. ____
80. ____
81. ____
82. ____
83. ____
84. ____
85. ____
86. ____
87. ____
88. ____
89. ____
90. ____
91. ____
92. ____
93. ____
94. ____
95. ____
96. ____
97. ____
98. ____
99. ____
100. ____

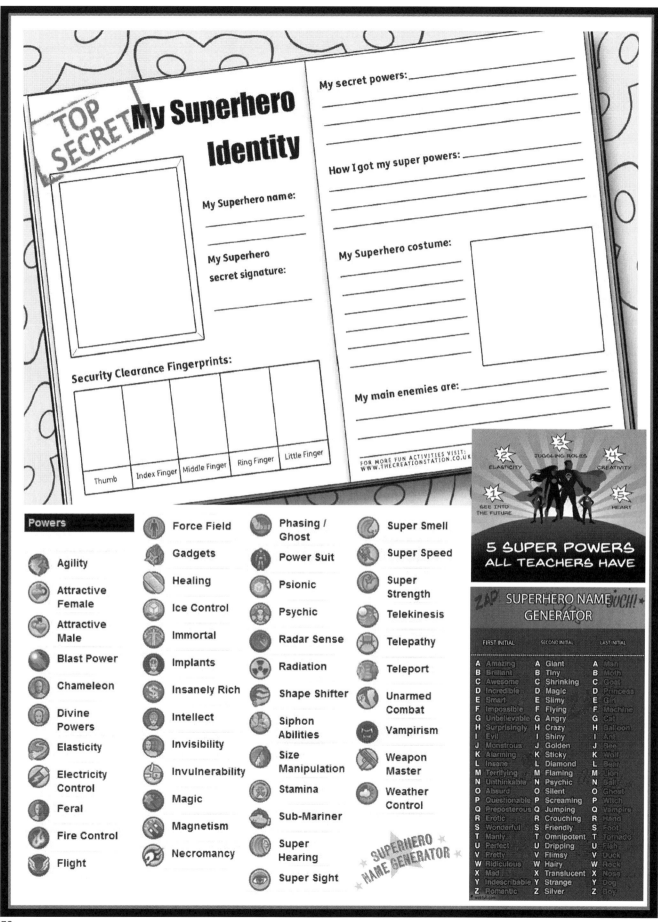

FINISH THESE DRAWING WITH RANDOM SELECTIONS FROM YOUR 100 THINGS LIST. CANNOT BE THE "NORMAL" HALF- BE CREATIVE.

FINISH THESE DRAWING WITH RANDOM SELECTIONS FROM YOUR 100 THINGS LIST. CANNOT BE THE "NORMAL" HALF- BE CREATIVE.

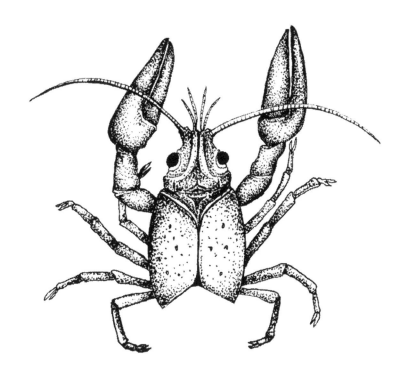

FINISH THESE DRAWING WITH RANDOM SELECTIONS FROM YOUR 100 THINGS LIST. CANNOT BE THE "NORMAL" HALF- BE CREATIVE.

CRITIQUE

BALOON DOG
JEFF KOONZ
2008 TO PRESENT
SCULPTURE
AV. PRICE $55 MILLION

DESCRIPTION
Describe this art as if you were talking to someone who couln't see it.

ANALASIS
what ELEMENTS of art are used to make the artwork?
LINE, COLOR, SHAPE, TEXTURE, FORM, VALUE, SACE
what PRINCIPALS of art are used to make the artwork?
EMPPHASIS, RHYTHM/MOVEMENT, UNITY REPETITION/PATTERN, CONTRAST/VARIETY, BALANCE, PROPORTION

INTERRETATION
1. Does the work make you think or feel?
2. Do you think this work was successful/why?
3. How does this work relate to the world you've experienced?

JUDGEMENT
1. Give your opinion on the works achievement or failure.
2. Is the work unique?
3. What could have improved the work?

DESCRIPTION, ANALASIS, INTERPRETATION, JUDGEMENT

D _____

A _____

I _____

J _____

Don't use lots of words... get to the point.

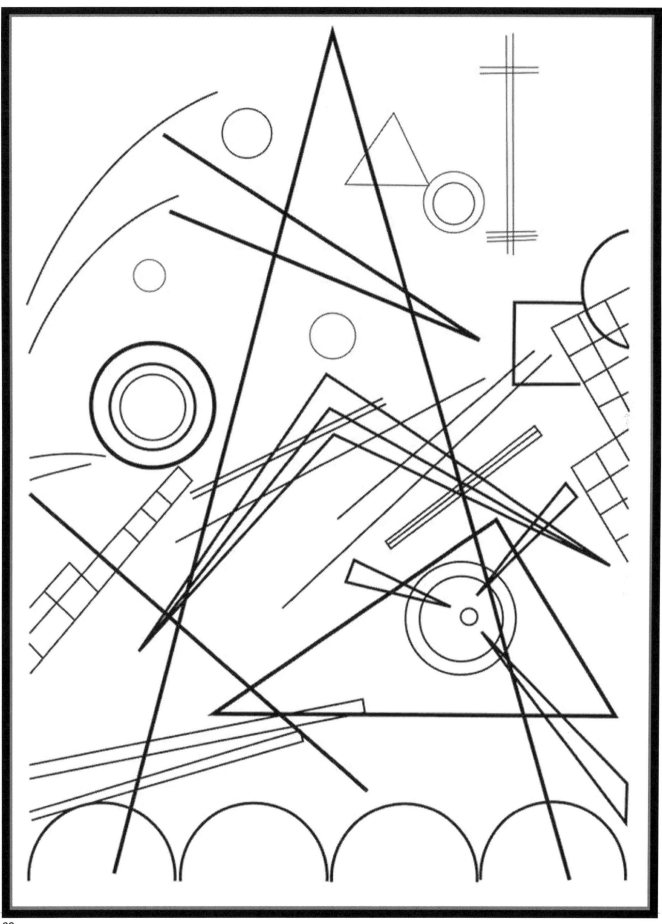

CRITIQUE

DESCRIPTION
Describe this art as if you were talking to someone who couln't see it.

ANALASIS
what ELEMENTS of art are used to make the artwork?
LINE, COLOR, SHAPE, TEXTURE, FORM, VALUE, SACE
what PRINCIPALS of art are used to make the artwork?
EMPPHASIS, RHYTHM/MOVEMENT, UNITY REPETITION/PATTERN, CONTRAST/VARIETY, BALANCE, PROPORTION

INTERRPETATION
1. Does the work make you think or feel?
2. Do you think this work was successful/why?
3. How does this work relate to the world you've experienced?

JUDGEMENT
1. Give your opinion on the works achievement or failure.
2. Is the work unique?
3. What could have improved the work?

DESCRIPTION, ANALASIS, INTERPRETATION, JUDGEMENT

D _____

A _____

I _____

J _____

Don't use lots of words... get to the point.

WARM-UP

ARTIST NAME
PIERRE-AUGUSTE RENOIR
ARTWORK NAME
DANCE IN BOUGIVAL
DATE OF ART
1882-3
NATIONALITY
FRENCH
BORN
1841
DIED
1919

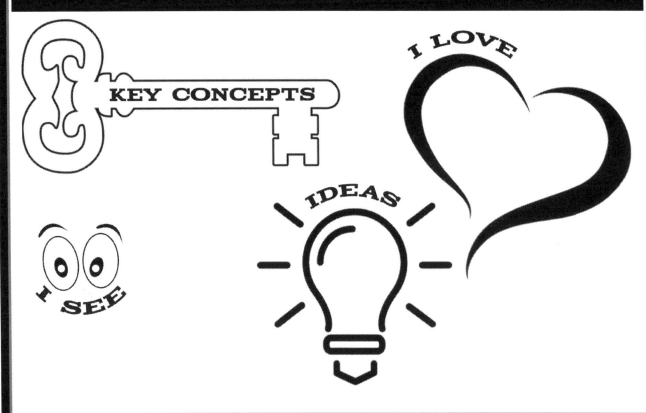

CREATIVITY
is intelligence
HAVING FUN

ART PRINCIPLES

PATTERN

IS THE REPETITION OF THE ELEMENTS OF ART OR ANYTHING ELSE.

PATTERNS OF LINE:

PATTERNS OF SHAPE:

PATTERNS OF COLOR:

NOTICE OTHER PATTERNS IN YOUR LIFE:
Breathing, Music, Math, Jumping Jacks, Butterfly Wings, Fabric, Habits . . .

PATTERN IS EVERYWHERE!

When I was a kid the painting American Gothic by Grant Wood was on the corn flakes box so we remembered it when we played the game Masterpiece. Whoever got it, treasured that painting most and if sold it went for the highest price.

THE ART OF PARODY: IMITATION WITH A TWIST

A PARODY IS AN IMITATION WITH A TWIST. IN OTHER WORDS, A GOOD PARODY IS A HUMOROUS OR IRONIC IMITATION OF ITS SOURCE. A GOOD PARODY SHOULD BE FUNNY, NOT RACIST OR BULLYING, OR INTOLERANT. BE NICE, BUT HAVE FUN. WHAT IS THE "MODERN" FORM OF PARODY

_____?

ART PARODY

NAME THE 7 ARTIST'S PARODIED HERE.
1.
2.
3.
4.
5.
6.
7.
TAKE A PICTURE OF THE ANSWERS, SEND TO ME AND GET 300 XP POINTS IN CLASSCRAFT....

60. **Grant Wood.** *American Gothic*, 1930.

WARM-UP

ARTIST NAME

GEORGES SEURAT

ARTWORK NAME

SUNDAY AFTERNOON...

DATE OF ART

1884-6

NATIONALITY

FRENCH

BORN

1859-1891

POINTILLISM-DOTS

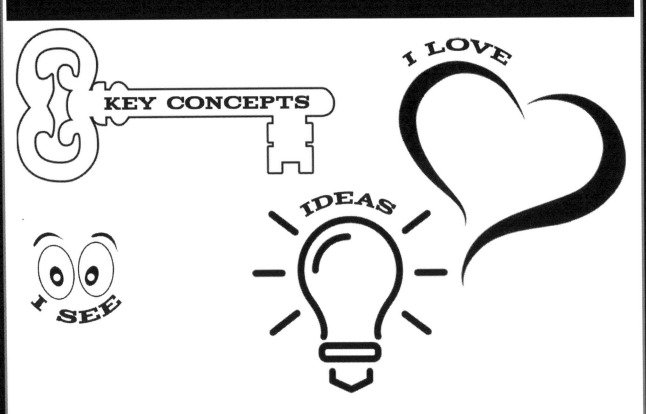

KEY CONCEPTS

I LOVE

I SEE

IDEAS

COMARE & CONTRAST

SIMILAR

1.
2.
3.
4.
5.

DIFFERENT

1.
2.
3.
4.
5.

GO DEEP- TAKE TIME TO THINK!

Iteration practice
Draw a different version of the object here in each square.

DEADLY	ROTTEN	MAGICAL
HAUNTED	EXPENSIVE	HOLIDAY
TALKING	VAMPIRE	FRIGHTENED

DRAW A PERSON'S FACE FROM MEMORY- DON'T LOOK AT ANYTHING.

DRAW SOMETHING FROM YOUR 100 THINGS LIST

DRAW SOMETHING FROM YOUR 100 THINGS LIST

DRAW SOMETHING FROM YOUR 100 THINGS LIST

DRAW SOMETHING FROM YOUR 100 THINGS LIST

WARM-UP

ARTIST NAME
ELIZABETH CATLETT

ARTWORK NAME
SHARECROPPER

DATE OF ART
1952

NATIONALITY
AFRICAN AMERICAN

BORN
1915-2012

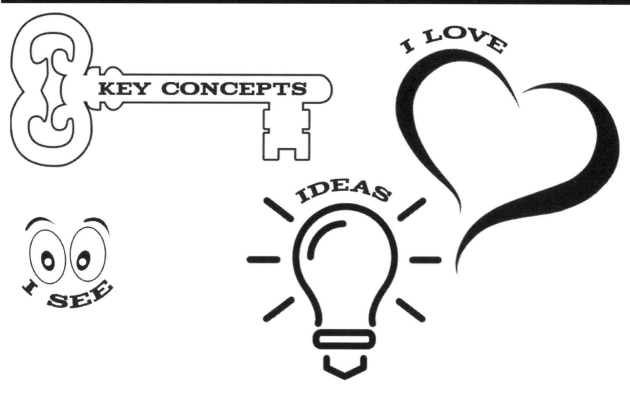

KEY CONCEPTS

I LOVE

I SEE

IDEAS

Iteration practice

Draw a different version of the object here in each square.

DEADLY	ROTTEN	MAGICAL
HAUNTED	EXPENSIVE	HOLIDAY
TALKING	VAMPIRE	FRIGHTENED

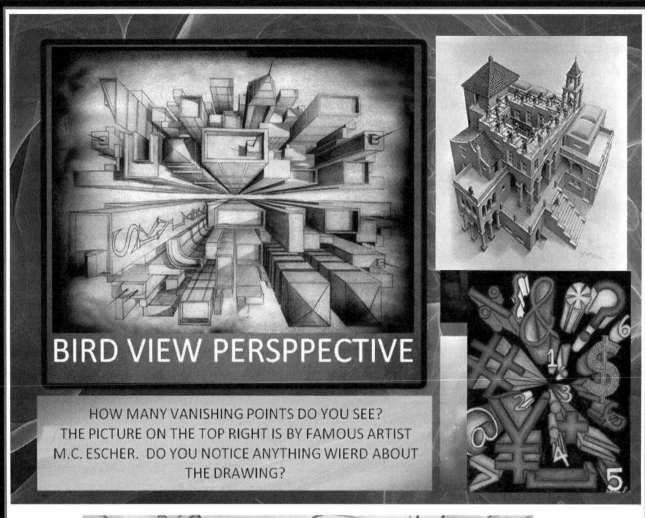
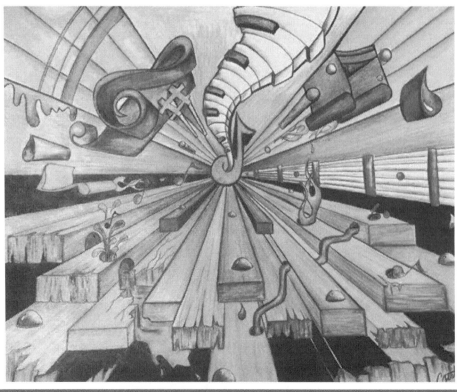

THE CHURCH AT AUVERS
Artist Vincent van Gogh
Year 1890
Type Oil on canvas
Dimensions
37 in × 29.1 in
Location
Musée d'Orsay, Paris

Post-impression was both an extension of impressionism and a rejection of its limitations. but post-impressionists aimed to get more emotion and expression into their paintings.

"Every ARTIST was first an amateur."

Ralph Waldo Emerson

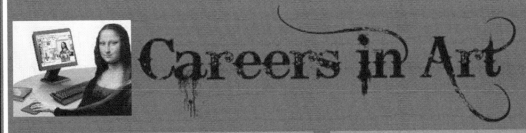

Careers in Art

GAME DESIGN
www.animationarena.com

- Project Manager
- Graphic Designer
- Lead Animator/Supporting Animators
- Game Designers
- Audio Engineer
- C+++ Programmer (aka Computer Programmer)
- Storyboard Creator
- Script Writer

A few main points to remember:
Keep drawing and don't copy other people's work, use it as a guide and learn from what they have done.
Don't be afraid of blank paper – just get in there and draw, nothing ever comes out right first time anyway.
Be critical of your art, and look hard at it to see what doesn't look right and then change weak aspects and improve on parts that already work within the illustration.

CAREER NAME GAME ART DESIGN

EDUCATION NEEDED
BACHELOR'S DEGREE MINIMUM
ART INSTITUTE- 2 ½ years $100,000

SALARY EXPECTATION
$45,000-$200,000

LOCATION http://gamedevmap.com/
82 COMPANIES IN AUSTIN, TX, 9 IN HOUSTON

PROS
GROWING INDUSTRY
GOOD SALARY
CREATIVE ENVIRONMENT

CONS INTENSE COMPETITION
NEED ADVANCED ARTISTIC ABILITY-
If your drawing skills are not strong
Consider the technical or writing division.

TOP TEN list — GAME DESIGN COMPANIES TO WORK FOR

1.
2.
3.
4.
5.
6.
7.
8.
9.
10.

THE BANJO LESSON

ARTISTS NAME:
HENRY O. TANNER
DATE OF ART:
1893
Oil on canvas,
49" × 35½".

"I was extremely timid and to be made to feel that I was not wanted, although in a place where I had every right to be, even months afterwards caused me sometimes weeks of pain. Every time any one of these disagreeable incidents came into my mind, my heart sank, and I was anew tortured by the thought of what I had endured, almost as much as the incident itself." - Tanner

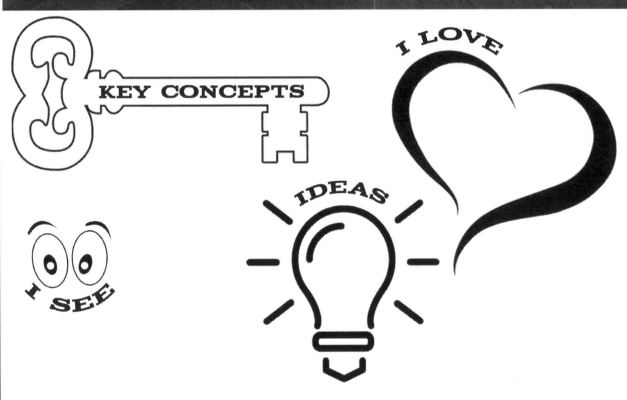

ARTIST

ARTIST NAME
JIM DINE

ARTWORK NAME
WATERCOLOR IN THE GALILEE

DATE OF ART
2001

NATIONALITY
AMERICAN

BORN
1935

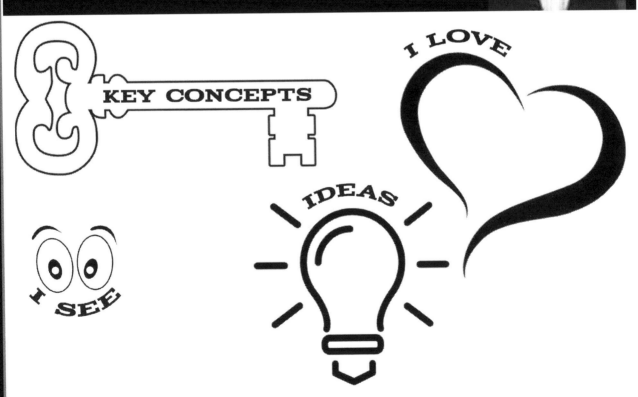

WARM-UP

ARTIST NAME
ROBERT INDIANA

ARTWORK NAME
LOVE

DATE OF ART
1968

NATIONALITY
AMERICAN
1928

KEY CONCEPTS

I LOVE

IDEAS

I SEE

113

DRAW SOMETHING FROM YOUR 100 THINGS LIST

ADVICE FOR COMIC BOOK ARTIST'S

1. DON'T HAVE PEOPLE JUST STANDING THERE.

2. ANY EXPRESSION IS BETTER THAN A BLANK STARE.

3. AVOID TANGENTS, AND ANY STRAIGHT LINE THAT DIVIDES THE PANEL.

4. IF YOU USE AN ODD ANGLE IN THE SHOT, THERE HAS TO BE A REASON FOR IT.

5. IF YOU DON'T HAVE AT LEAST ONE PANEL ON EACH PAGE WITH A FULL FIGURE, YOUR "CAMERA" IS TOO CLOSE.

6. PLAN OUT YOUR SHOTS IN "JURASSIC PARK" MODE RATHER THAN IN "FOX NEWS" MODE.

7. DON'T THINK OF BACKGROUNDS AS "THINGS TO FILL UP THE SPACE AFTER THE FIGURES ARE DRAWN."

8. IF YOU KNOW WHAT SOMETHING IS CALLED, AND YOU HAVE AN INTERNET CONNECTION, THERE IS NO REASON TO DRAW IT INACCURATELY.

9. IF THE COLORIST HAS TO ASK IF A SCENE TAKES PLACE AT NIGHT, YOU HAVEN'T DONE YOUR JOB.

10. IF YOU CAN'T EXTEND THE DRAWING BEYOND THE PANEL BORDERS AND STILL HAVE IT MAKE VISUAL SENSE, YOU'VE CHEATED ON THE PERSPECTIVE!!

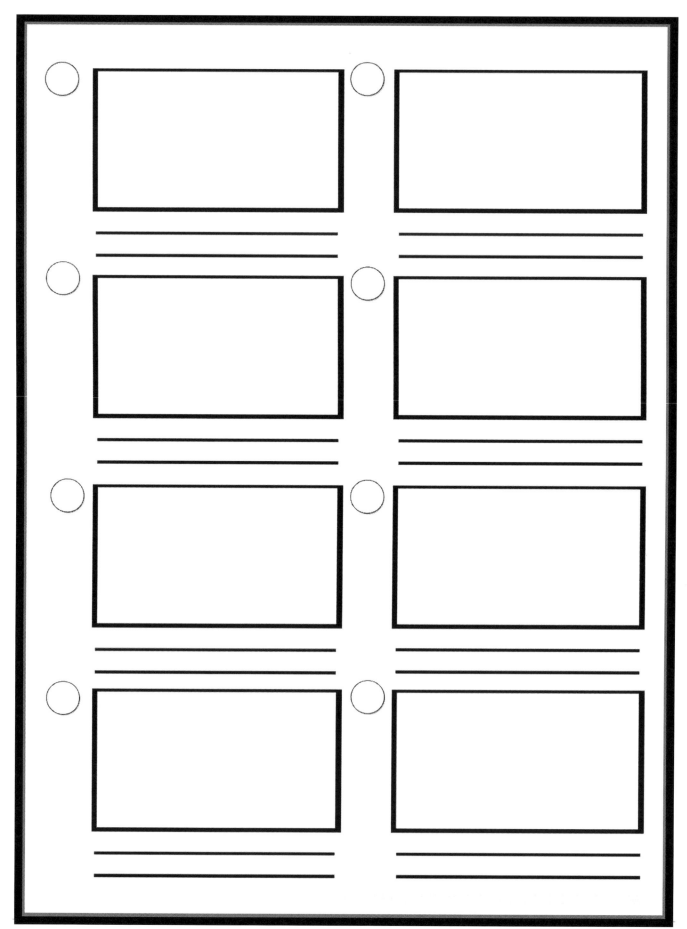

ARTIST NAME
ROY LICHTENSTEIN

ARTWORK NAME.... WHAM

DATE OF ART....1967

NATIONALITY.... AMERICAN

1923-1997

Find out how big the painting "Wham"
is _____ x _____ INCHES

Who owns it now?

_____

"ART DOESN'T TRANSFORM IT JUST PLAIN FORMS"
- ROY LICHTENSTEIN

Pop Art is the use of commercial art as a subject matter in painting. I suppose. It was hard to get a painting that was despicable enough so that no one would hang it - everybody was hanging everything. It was almost acceptable to hang a dripping paint rag, everybody [in America, mainly in New York, 1950s] was accustomed to this. The one thing everyone hated was commercial art: and apparently they didn't hate that enough either.

- Roy Lichtenstein

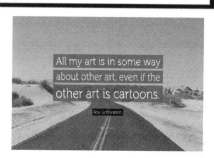

All my art is in some way about other art, even if the other art is cartoons.
Roy Lichtenstein

WARM-UP

ARTIST NAME
PABLO PICASSO
ARTWORK NAME
WOMAN IN A HAIRNET
DATE OF ART
1938
NATIONALITY
SPANISH
BORN
1881
DIED
1973

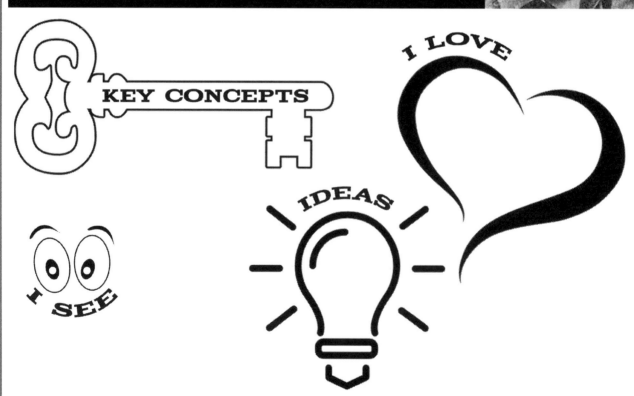

KEY CONCEPTS

I LOVE

I SEE

IDEAS

Iteration practice
Draw a different version of the object here in each square.

DEADLY	ROTTEN	MAGICAL
HAUNTED	EXPENSIVE	HOLIDAY
TALKING	VAMPIRE	FRIGHTENED

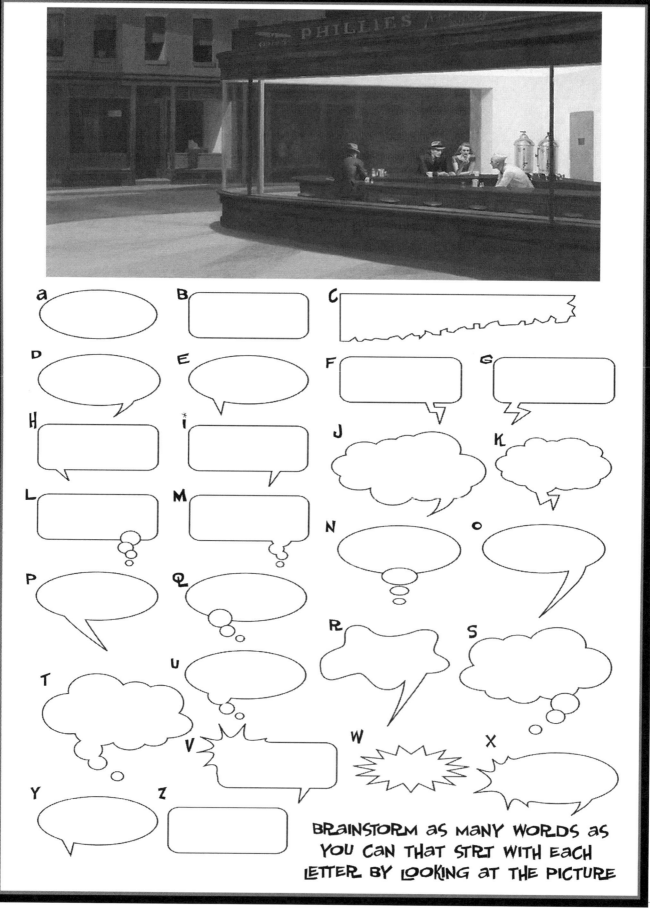

Edward Hopper created "Nighthawks"

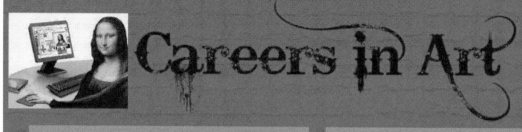
Careers in Art

ARCHITECTURE

Architects design buildings and other structures. In addition to considering the way these buildings and structures look, they also make sure they are functional, safe, economical and suit the needs of the people who use them.

CAREER NAME
 Architectural engineer

EDUCATION NEEDED
 4 year Bachelor' degree minimum
 6-8 year Master's degree

SALARY EXPECTATION
 $41,000-$62,000 AVG
 EXTREME END EARN MILIONS

LOCATION
 WORLDWIDE

PROS
 21% SELF-EMPLOYED
 TRAVEL
 CREATIVE FREEDOM

CONS
 INTENSE COMPETITION
 LONG TRAINING/EDUCATION
 CREATIVE COMPROMISE FOR CLIENTS

TOP TeN list — FAMOUS ARCHITECTS OF THE WORLD

1.
2.
3.
4.
5.

6.
7.
8.
9.
10.

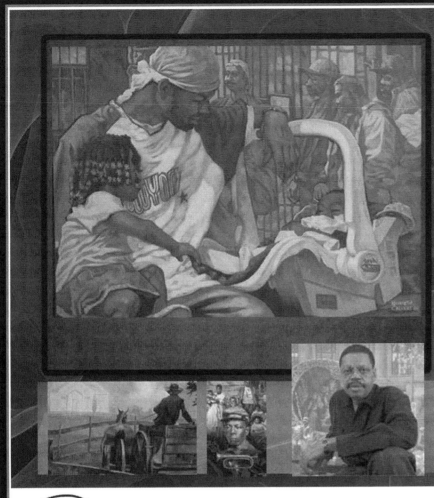

FATHERHOOD

ARTIST
KENNETH CALVERT
B-1932
ORIGINAL ART
$4030
ALSO SOLD AS PRINTS IN VARIOUS SIZES
2006

Statement: "My work is an exploratory journey through a range of perceptual challenges. I accept no limitation in terms of subject matter or mode of expression. Instead I prefer to exist in a state of constant expansion in many creative directions, with my academic foundation serving as the unifying element in each of my works. This approach, I refer to as "Controlled Diversity".

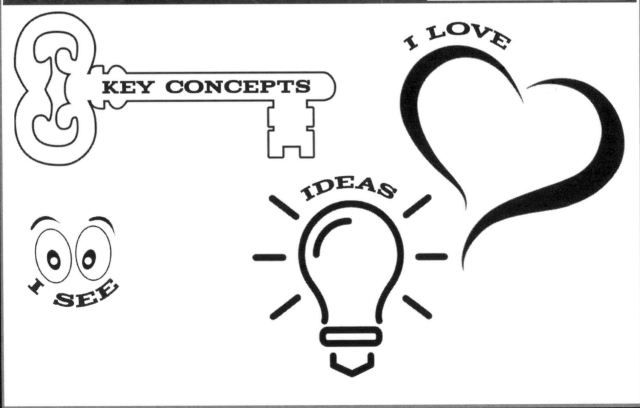

Design Principles
Planning and organizing tools for art.

MOVEMENT

BALANCE

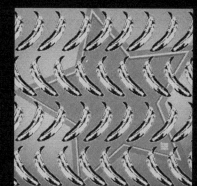

CONTRAST

PATTERN

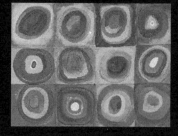

UNITY

EMPHASIS

RHYTHM

Design Principles

DRAW LINES TO DIAGRAM THE PRINCIPLES IN THIS M.C. ESCHER ART

MOVEMENT   PATTERN   CONTRAST

BALANCE   RHYTHM   UNITY   EMPHASIS

Tesselations

It's like puzzles where every piece is shaped the same.

At least in it's most simple form.. like the ones ABOVE.
BUT it can get more complicated.
These examples are from the arist M.C.Escher

Tesselations

An easy way to visualize and create a tesselation.

cut out a square

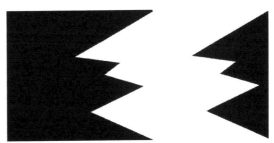
Cut a piece off of it

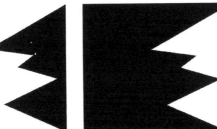

Move the cut off piece to the oposie side- DON'T flip it-tape it together..

Trace the shape over and over to create a pattern and color it.

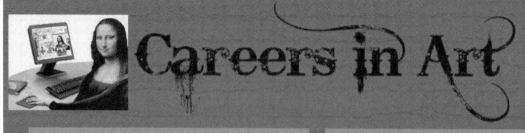
Careers in Art

TEACHER

At a minimum, art teachers are generally required to have a Bachelor of Fine Arts or similar degree in addition to a teaching certification, in order to enter the career field. At the postsecondary level, teachers need to have a master's degree and possibly higher in some cases. Art teaching degrees can focus on one or more of the following art spheres:
Ceramics
Painting
Sculpture
Media arts
Drawing
Photography
Graphic design
Upon graduation, many students complete a one-year internship in schools, equivalent to a first year of teaching. Public schools require licensure in art education before teachers may lead a classroom on their own.

CAREER NAME
  ART INSTRUCTOR

EDUCATION NEEDED
  4 YEAR COLLEGE MINIMUM

SALARY EXPECTATION
  $35,000-$65,000

LOCATION
  WORLDWIDE

PROS
  SUMMERS OFF
  HELPING STUDENTS
  CREATIVE ENVIRONMENT

CONS
  INCOME CAP
  STRESS
  CRATIVE CONSTRAINT

TOP TEN list EXCUSES YOU'VE GIVEN TEACHERS...

1.
2.
3.
4.
5.
6.
7.
8.
9.
10.

Doodling-on purpose

I am sure you have mindlessly doodled while listening to your history teacher drone on about something historically snozeworthy.

DOODLE-AWAY

"Manchester Doodle Bee"
Part of the Bee in the City project, sponsored by Transport for Greater Manchester, designed and decorated by Dave Draws and sited on Piccadilly Station Approach. The artist's work is map-based and is built on picking out 'hotspots' that are dotted around the city.

Some Day your DOODLES could grow up to be DOODLE BEES

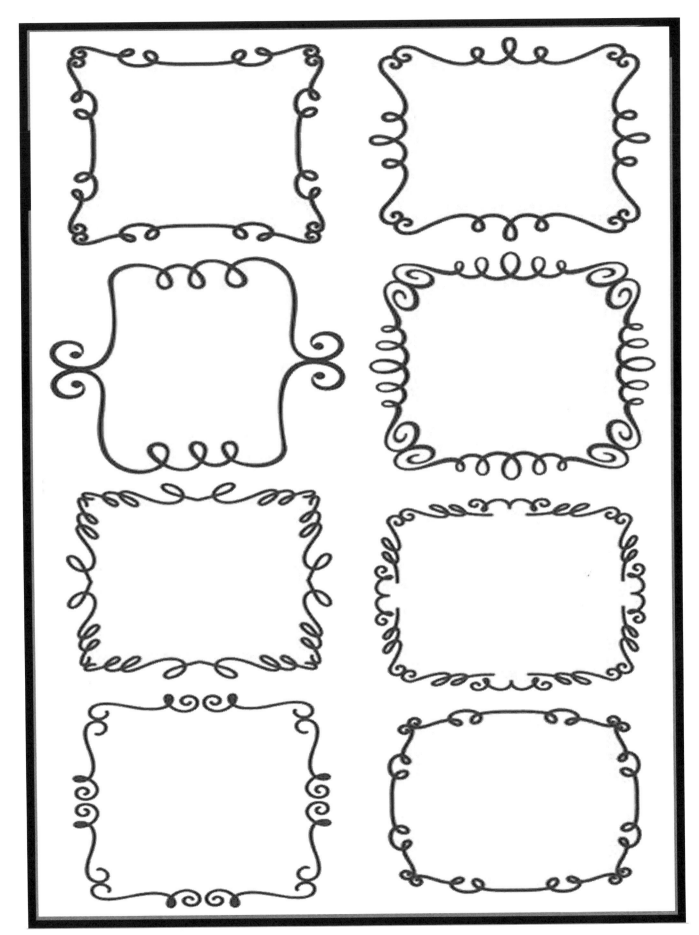

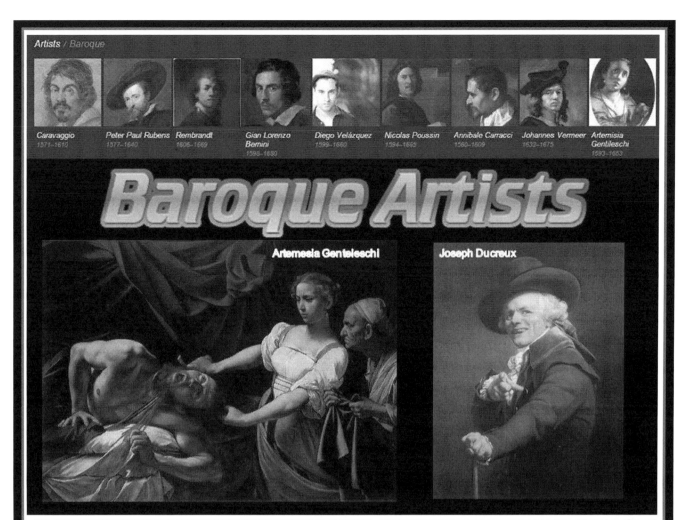
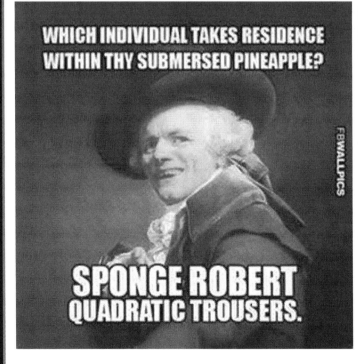
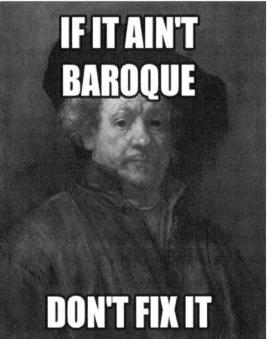

WRITE 2 RANDOM NUMBERS HERE _____ & _____
GO BACK TO THE LIST OF 100 THINGS...DON'T CHEAT!!
DRAW THE RANDOM PAIRS AS A MASH-UP

@KYLESTYL3

HERE IS A GREAT YOUNG ARTIST TO FOLLOW- ENJOY HIS STYLE AND THEN CREATE YOUR OWN. DON'T JUST COPY. THAT'S WHY IT'S GREAT TO USE YOUR 100 THINGS LIST.

MASH-UP ART

MASH-UP ART

MASH-UP ART

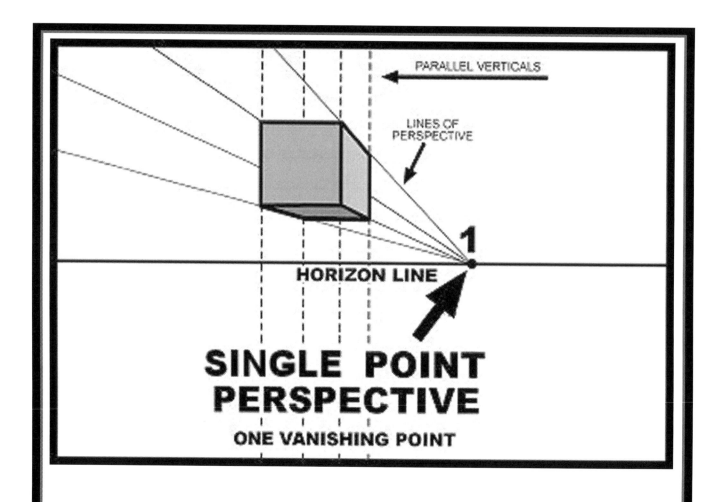

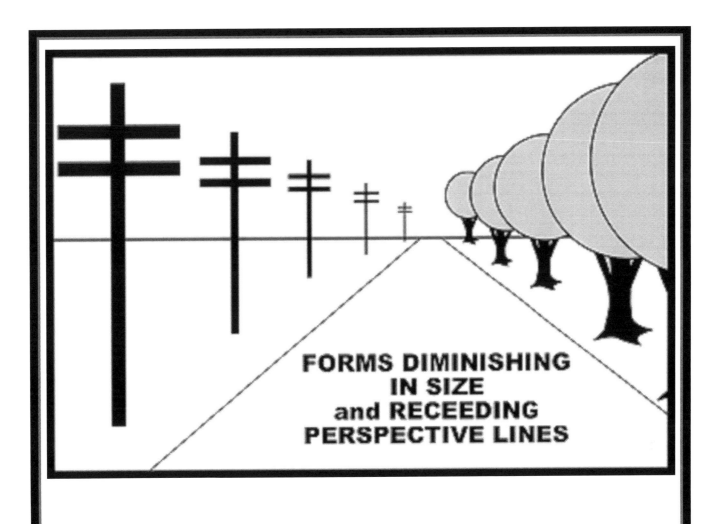

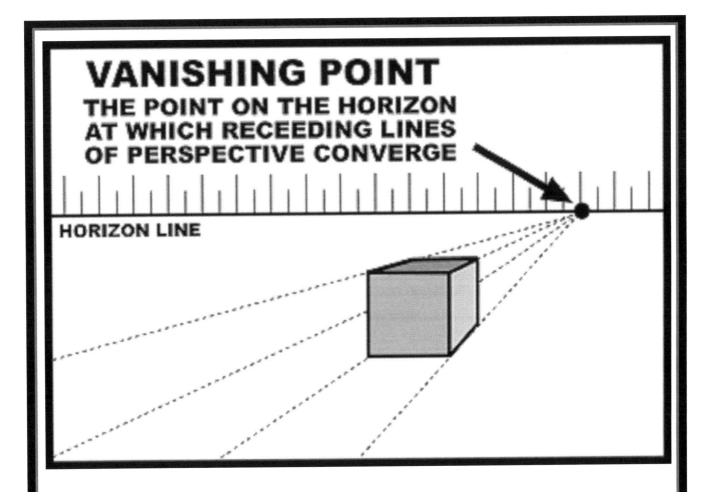

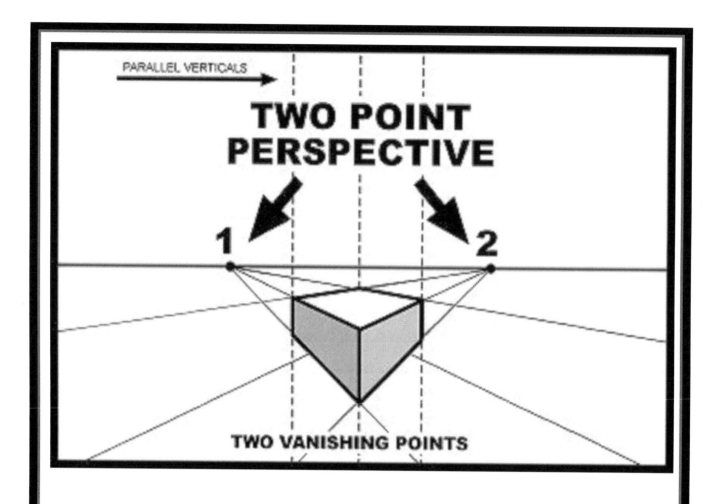

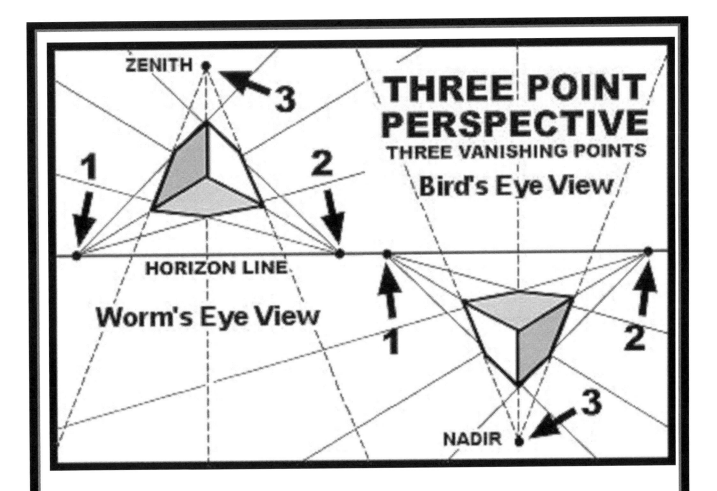

WARM-UP

ARTIST NAME
EDVARD MUNCH

ARTWORK NAME
THE SCREAM

DATE OF ART
1893

NATIONALITY
NORWEIGIAN

BORN
1863

DIED
1944

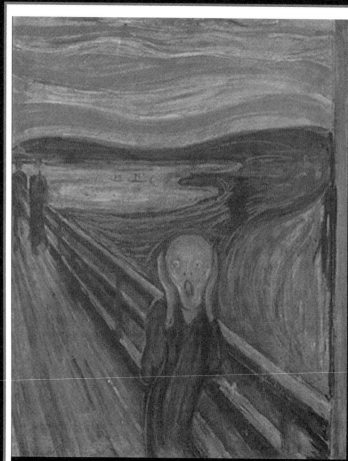

"Death is pitch-dark, but colors are light. To be a painter, one must work with rays of light."

Edvard Munch

Artist, Sophia Sanhueza
@SofiaSanhuezaart

Sophia was my art student for 4 years

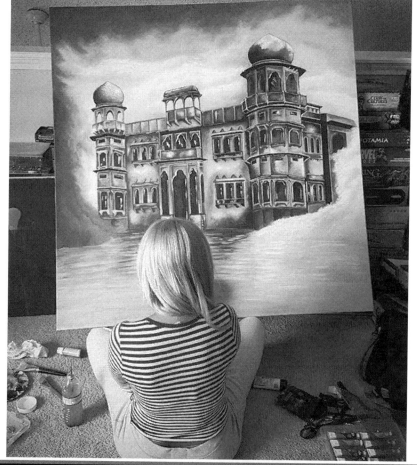

"Art enables us to find ourselves and lose ourselves at the same time" -Sofia

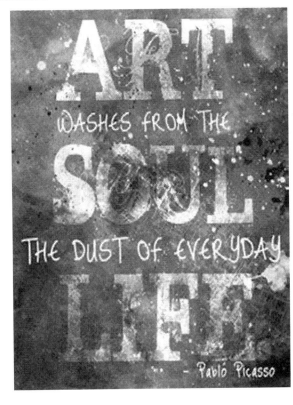

An artist asked the gallery owner if there had been any interest in his paintings on display at that time.
"I have good news and bad news," the owner replied. "The good news is that a gentleman enquired about your work and wondered if it would appreciate in value after your death. When I told him it would, he bought all 15 of your paintings."

"That's wonderful," the artist exclaimed. "What's the bad news?"
"The guy was your doctor..."

DRAW SOMETHING FROM YOUR 100 THINGS LIST

DRAW SOMETHING FROM YOUR 100 THINGS LIST

DRAW SOMETHING FROM YOUR 100 THINGS LIST

DRAW SOMETHING FROM YOUR 100 THINGS LIST

DRAW SOMETHING FROM YOUR 100 THINGS LIST

DRAW SOMETHING FROM YOUR 100 THINGS LIST

DRAW SOMETHING FROM YOUR 100 THINGS LIST

Iteration practice

Draw a different version of the object here in each square.

DEADLY	ROTTEN	MAGICAL
HAUNTED	EXPENSIVE	HOLIDAY
TALKING	VAMPIRE	FRIGHTENED

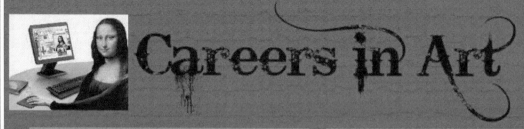

Careers in Art

TATTOO ARTIST

- Consult with client about ideas and possibilities for artwork
- Explain the tattooing procedure to the client
- May gain written consent from a client
- May design new image for client
- Create an image stencil
- Prepare tattooing area by shaving and disinfecting skin
- Using stencil, outline, color, and shadow the tattoo with inked needles
- Cover finished tattoo with antiseptic and bandages
- Explain proper care of tattoos
- Sterilize all equipment
- May work as a piercer as well as a tattoo artist
- May manage shop
- Tattoo artists spend most of each day meeting with potential clients, discussing possible designs and locations for tattoos. They may complete only one tattoo a day, or they may work on 10. Most time not spent tattooing is spent creating sample designs, contacting clients to check up on the healing process, ordering supplies, and performing administrative duties, such as looking after finances and creating advertising opportunities.

CAREER NAME TATTOO ARTIST-DESIGNER

EDUCATION NEEDED SOME ART SCHOOL, INTERNSHIP, PORTFOLIO, SOME GO TO A SPECIALIZE SCHOOL
http://tattoo-school.com/

SALARY EXPECTATION $14,000-$65,000

LOCATION anywhere

PROS
- SELF-EXPRESSION
- OPORTUNITY TO MENTOR OTHERS
- HUMAN INTERATION

CONS
- YEARS OF TRAINING
- HIGH EXPENSES
- INTENSE COMPETITION
- LOW PROFIT MARGIN

TOP TEN list: EXCUSES FOR MESSING UP A CUSTOMER'S TATTOO!

1.
2.
3.
4.
5.
6.
7.
8.
9.
10.

DRAW SOMETHING FROM YOUR 100 THINGS LIST

COMARE & CONTRAST

SIMILAR

1.
2.
3.
4.
5.

DIFFERENT

1.
2.
3.
4.
5.

GO DEEP- TAKE TIME TO THINK!

DRAW SOMETHING FROM YOUR 100 THINGS LIST

DRAW SOMETHING FROM YOUR 100 THINGS LIST

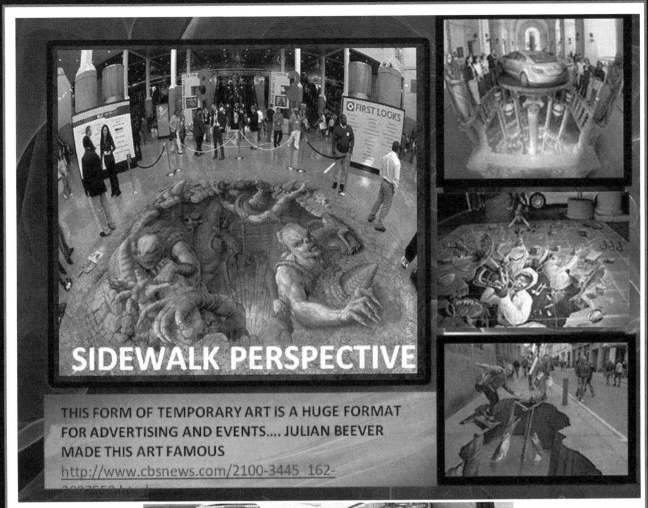

SIDEWALK PERSPECTIVE

THIS FORM OF TEMPORARY ART IS A HUGE FORMAT FOR ADVERTISING AND EVENTS.... JULIAN BEEVER MADE THIS ART FAMOUS

http://www.cbsnews.com/2100-3445_162-

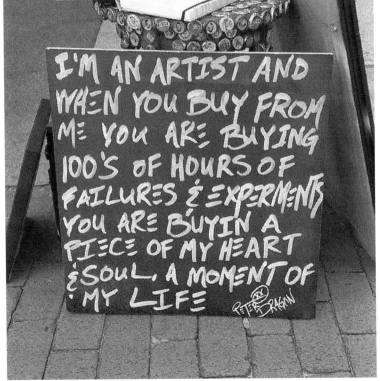

I'M AN ARTIST AND WHEN YOU BUY FROM ME YOU ARE BUYING 100'S OF HOURS OF FAILURES & EXPERIMENTS YOU ARE BUYIN A PIECE OF MY HEART & SOUL, A MOMENT OF MY LIFE

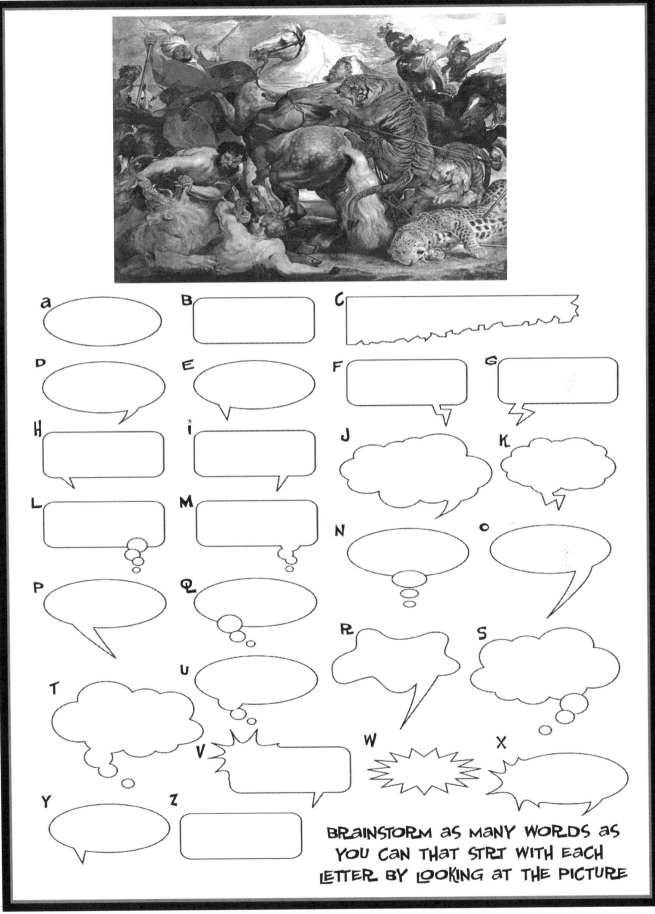

Peter Paul Rubens "The Tiger Chase"

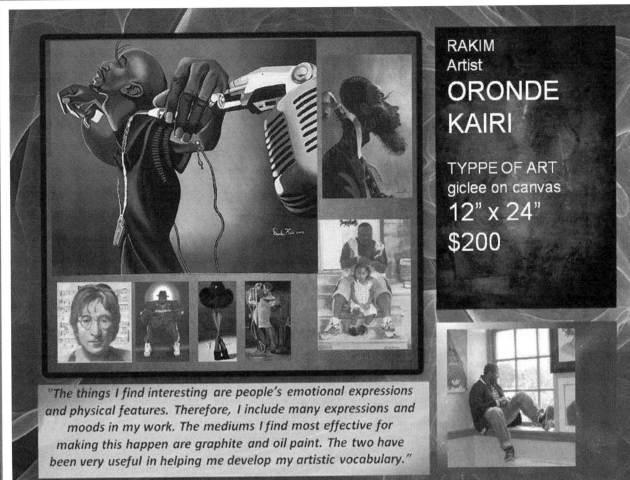

RAKIM
Artist

ORONDE KAIRI

TYPPE OF ART
giclee on canvas

12" x 24"

$200

"The things I find interesting are people's emotional expressions and physical features. Therefore, I include many expressions and moods in my work. The mediums I find most effective for making this happen are graphite and oil paint. The two have been very useful in helping me develop my artistic vocabulary."

WHAT INSPIRES YOU?

MURALIST

What could be more thrilling for an artist than to see their work displayed on a massive canvas, for an entire community to admire? A successful muralist is a fine artist, but also an individual who has a keen sense of scale and dimension. Expand your dream by learning what it takes to be a muralist.

Mural in Houston, about Galveston

To get a price estimate, multiply the square footage times the cost per square foot. Prices range from $10 to $20 per square foot for wall murals. A 50 square foot wall at the lowest price (low detail) is $500.00. At the highest price (high detail), the same wall would cost $1500.00.

OH, WAIT- PABLO PICASSO PAINTED LIKE THAT ALL THE TIME AND HE WAS FAMOUS!

"Every child is an artist. The problem is how to remain an artist once we grow up"
- Pablo Picasso

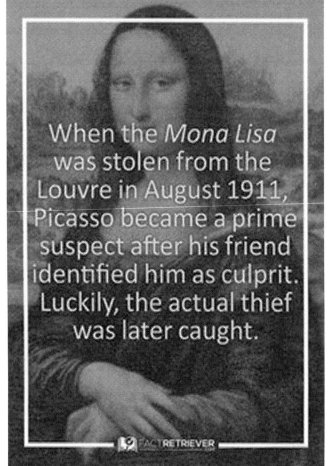

When the Mona Lisa was stolen from the Louvre in August 1911, Picasso became a prime suspect after his friend identified him as culprit. Luckily, the actual thief was later caught.

LADY CRASHED INTO THIS PAINTING

"The Actor"
Artist: Pablo Picasso
72" x 48" oil painting
Worth 130 million (before tear)

THIS IS THE MAN WHO ACTUALLY STOLE MONA LISA

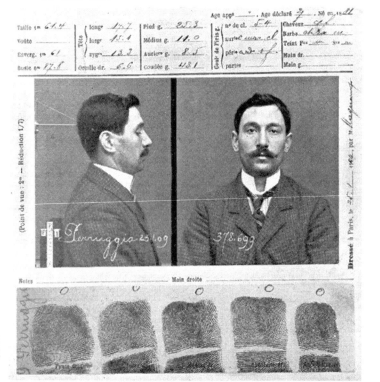

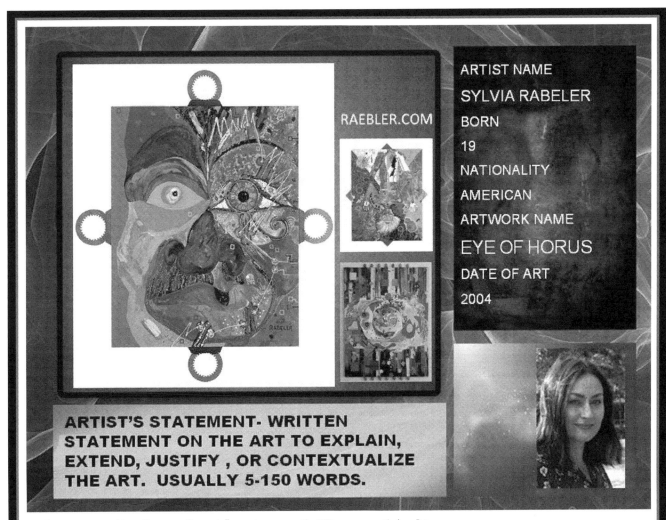

LIST 20 WORDS THAT DESCRIBE YOU

Make Your Own Meme

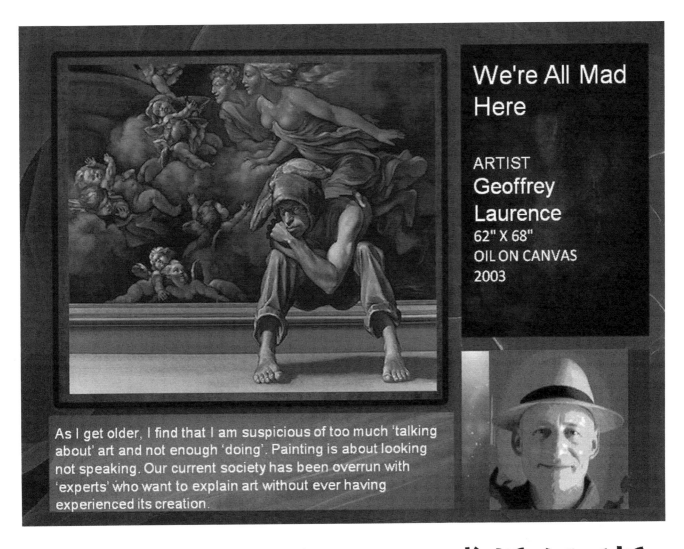

WRITE A BLURB FOR A BOOK USING THIS PAINTING AS INSPIRATION

CREATE A BOOK COVER

DRAW SOMETHING FROM YOUR 100 THINGS LIST

DRAW SOMETHING FROM YOUR 100 THINGS LIST

DRAW SOMETHING FROM YOUR 100 THINGS LIST

KEEP DRAWING...
REMEMBER.....

AN ERASER IS LIKE TRAINING WHEELS
TRACING IS BEST FOR ENLARGING WHAT YOU ACTUALLY DREW
DRAW LIGHT
LET YOUR PICTURES RUN OFF THE PAGES
IF IT'S EASY YOU AREN'T CHALLENGING YOURSELF- PROBABLY
DRAW ALL KINDS OF THINGS
ACTUALLY LOOK AT REAL STUFF TO DRAW IT
IF YOU "BORROW" AN IDEA- CHANGE IT AND MAKE IT BETTER
BOOGERS... JUST SEEING IF YOU WERE READING
ART AS A HOBBY CAN KEEP LAWYERS/DOCTORS HAPPY
YOU CAN DO IT
YES, THE JUNK IN THE MUSEUM LOOKS LIKE A 4 YEAR OLD DID IT
NO ONE IS IMPRESSED WITH YOUR "MISSLE" DRAWINGS- JUST STOP
GOT YA THERE!
LUV YA!
-ART GYPSY LESLIE BROWN

Copyrigt 2018
Leslie Brown

www.ArtGypsyDecals.com

Made in the USA
Middletown, DE
13 September 2022